Daily Gratitude

JOURNAL

This Journal Belongs To:

_____

Today I Am Grateful For

_____

_____

_____

_____

_____

_____

_____

_____

_____

_____

_____

_____

_____

_____

_____

_____

_____

_____

_____

_____

1

"It's not happiness that brings us gratitude.
It's gratitude that brings us happiness."
— Anonymous

Today I Am Grateful For

"It's not happiness that brings us gratitude.
It's gratitude that brings us happiness."
— Anonymous

Today I Am Grateful For

"It's not happiness that brings us gratitude.
It's gratitude that brings us happiness."
— Anonymous

Today I Am Grateful For

_____

_____

_____

_____

_____

_____

_____

_____

_____

_____

_____

_____

_____

_____

_____

_____

_____

_____

_____

_____

"It's not happiness that brings us gratitude.
It's gratitude that brings us happiness."
— Anonymous

Today I Am Grateful For

_____

_____

_____

_____

_____

_____

_____

_____

_____

_____

_____

_____

_____

_____

_____

_____

_____

_____

_____

_____

_____

_____

"It's not happiness that brings us gratitude.
It's gratitude that brings us happiness."
— Anonymous

Today I Am Grateful For

_____

_____

_____

_____

_____

_____

_____

_____

_____

_____

_____

_____

_____

_____

_____

_____

_____

_____

_____

_____

"It's not happiness that brings us gratitude.
It's gratitude that brings us happiness."
— Anonymous

Today I Am Grateful For

_____

_____

_____

_____

_____

_____

_____

_____

_____

_____

_____

_____

_____

_____

_____

_____

_____

_____

7

"It's not happiness that brings us gratitude.
It's gratitude that brings us happiness."
— Anonymous

Today I Am Grateful For

_____

_____

_____

_____

_____

_____

_____

_____

_____

_____

_____

_____

_____

_____

_____

_____

_____

_____

_____

"It's not happiness that brings us gratitude.
It's gratitude that brings us happiness."
— Anonymous

Today I Am Grateful For

_____

_____

_____

_____

_____

_____

_____

_____

_____

_____

_____

_____

_____

_____

_____

_____

_____

_____

_____

"It's not happiness that brings us gratitude.
It's gratitude that brings us happiness."
— Anonymous

Today I Am Grateful For

_____

_____

_____

_____

_____

_____

_____

_____

_____

_____

_____

_____

_____

_____

_____

_____

_____

_____

_____

"It's not happiness that brings us gratitude.
It's gratitude that brings us happiness."
— Anonymous

Today I Am Grateful For

_____

_____

_____

_____

_____

_____

_____

_____

_____

_____

_____

_____

_____

_____

_____

_____

_____

_____

_____

_____

"It's not happiness that brings us gratitude.
It's gratitude that brings us happiness."
— Anonymous

Today I Am Grateful For

_____

_____

_____

_____

_____

_____

_____

_____

_____

_____

_____

_____

_____

_____

_____

_____

_____

_____

"It's not happiness that brings us gratitude.
It's gratitude that brings us happiness."
— Anonymous

Today I Am Grateful For

"It's not happiness that brings us gratitude.
It's gratitude that brings us happiness."
— Anonymous

Today I Am Grateful For

_____
_____
_____
_____
_____
_____
_____
_____
_____
_____
_____
_____
_____
_____
_____
_____
_____
_____
_____
_____

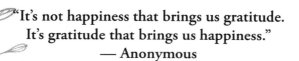

"It's not happiness that brings us gratitude.
It's gratitude that brings us happiness."
— Anonymous

Today I Am Grateful For

_____

_____

_____

_____

_____

_____

_____

_____

_____

_____

_____

_____

_____

_____

_____

_____

_____

_____

_____

"It's not happiness that brings us gratitude.
It's gratitude that brings us happiness."
— Anonymous

Today I Am Grateful For

_____

_____

_____

_____

_____

_____

_____

_____

_____

_____

_____

_____

_____

_____

_____

_____

_____

_____

_____

_____

"It's not happiness that brings us gratitude.
It's gratitude that brings us happiness."
— Anonymous

Today I Am Grateful For

_____

_____

_____

_____

_____

_____

_____

_____

_____

_____

_____

_____

_____

_____

_____

_____

_____

_____

_____

_____

"It's not happiness that brings us gratitude.
It's gratitude that brings us happiness."
— Anonymous

Today I Am Grateful For

_____

_____

_____

_____

_____

_____

_____

_____

_____

_____

_____

_____

_____

_____

_____

_____

_____

_____

_____

"It's not happiness that brings us gratitude.
It's gratitude that brings us happiness."
— Anonymous

Today I Am Grateful For

_____

_____

_____

_____

_____

_____

_____

_____

_____

_____

_____

_____

_____

_____

_____

_____

_____

_____

_____

_____

"It's not happiness that brings us gratitude.
It's gratitude that brings us happiness."
— Anonymous

Today I Am Grateful For

_____

_____

_____

_____

_____

_____

_____

_____

_____

_____

_____

_____

_____

_____

_____

_____

_____

_____

_____

"It's not happiness that brings us gratitude.
It's gratitude that brings us happiness."
— Anonymous

Today I Am Grateful For

"It's not happiness that brings us gratitude.
It's gratitude that brings us happiness."
— Anonymous

Today I Am Grateful For

_____

_____

_____

_____

_____

_____

_____

_____

_____

_____

_____

_____

_____

_____

_____

_____

_____

_____

_____

_____

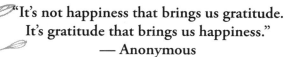

"It's not happiness that brings us gratitude.
It's gratitude that brings us happiness."
— Anonymous

Today I Am Grateful For

_____

_____

_____

_____

_____

_____

_____

_____

_____

_____

_____

_____

_____

_____

_____

_____

_____

_____

_____

_____

"It's not happiness that brings us gratitude.
It's gratitude that brings us happiness."
— Anonymous

Today I Am Grateful For

_____

_____

_____

_____

_____

_____

_____

_____

_____

_____

_____

_____

_____

_____

_____

_____

_____

_____

"It's not happiness that brings us gratitude.
It's gratitude that brings us happiness."
— Anonymous

Today I Am Grateful For

_____

_____

_____

_____

_____

_____

_____

_____

_____

_____

_____

_____

_____

_____

_____

_____

_____

_____

_____

"It's not happiness that brings us gratitude.
It's gratitude that brings us happiness."
— Anonymous

Today I Am Grateful For

_____
_____
_____
_____
_____
_____
_____
_____
_____
_____
_____
_____
_____
_____
_____
_____
_____
_____

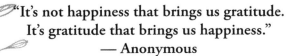

"It's not happiness that brings us gratitude.
It's gratitude that brings us happiness."
— Anonymous

Today I Am Grateful For

_____

_____

_____

_____

_____

_____

_____

_____

_____

_____

_____

_____

_____

_____

_____

_____

_____

_____

"It's not happiness that brings us gratitude.
It's gratitude that brings us happiness."
— Anonymous

Today I Am Grateful For

_____

_____

_____

_____

_____

_____

_____

_____

_____

_____

_____

_____

_____

_____

_____

_____

_____

_____

_____

_____

"It's not happiness that brings us gratitude.
It's gratitude that brings us happiness."
— Anonymous

28

Today I Am Grateful For

_____

_____

_____

_____

_____

_____

_____

_____

_____

_____

_____

_____

_____

_____

_____

_____

_____

_____

_____

_____

"It's not happiness that brings us gratitude.
It's gratitude that brings us happiness."
— Anonymous

Today I Am Grateful For

"It's not happiness that brings us gratitude.
It's gratitude that brings us happiness."
— Anonymous

30

Today I Am Grateful For

_____

_____

_____

_____

_____

_____

_____

_____

_____

_____

_____

_____

_____

_____

_____

_____

_____

_____

"It's not happiness that brings us gratitude.
It's gratitude that brings us happiness."
— Anonymous

Today I Am Grateful For

"It's not happiness that brings us gratitude.
It's gratitude that brings us happiness."
— Anonymous

Today I Am Grateful For

_____

_____

_____

_____

_____

_____

_____

_____

_____

_____

_____

_____

_____

_____

_____

_____

_____

_____

"It's not happiness that brings us gratitude.
It's gratitude that brings us happiness."
— Anonymous

Today I Am Grateful For

_____
_____
_____
_____
_____
_____
_____
_____
_____
_____
_____
_____
_____
_____
_____
_____
_____
_____
_____
_____
_____
_____

"It's not happiness that brings us gratitude.
It's gratitude that brings us happiness."
— Anonymous

Today I Am Grateful For

_____

_____

_____

_____

_____

_____

_____

_____

_____

_____

_____

_____

_____

_____

_____

_____

_____

_____

_____

_____

"It's not happiness that brings us gratitude.
It's gratitude that brings us happiness."
— Anonymous

Today I Am Grateful For

_____

_____

_____

_____

_____

_____

_____

_____

_____

_____

_____

_____

_____

_____

_____

_____

_____

_____

"It's not happiness that brings us gratitude.
It's gratitude that brings us happiness."
— Anonymous

36

Today I Am Grateful For

_____

_____

_____

_____

_____

_____

_____

_____

_____

_____

_____

_____

_____

_____

_____

_____

_____

_____

_____

_____

"It's not happiness that brings us gratitude.
It's gratitude that brings us happiness."
— Anonymous

Today I Am Grateful For

_____

_____

_____

_____

_____

_____

_____

_____

_____

_____

_____

_____

_____

_____

_____

_____

_____

_____

"It's not happiness that brings us gratitude.
It's gratitude that brings us happiness."
— Anonymous

Today I Am Grateful For

"It's not happiness that brings us gratitude.
It's gratitude that brings us happiness."
— Anonymous

Today I Am Grateful For

_____

_____

_____

_____

_____

_____

_____

_____

_____

_____

_____

_____

_____

_____

_____

_____

_____

_____

_____

_____

"It's not happiness that brings us gratitude.
It's gratitude that brings us happiness."
— Anonymous

Today I Am Grateful For

_____

_____

_____

_____

_____

_____

_____

_____

_____

_____

_____

_____

_____

_____

_____

_____

_____

_____

_____

_____

"It's not happiness that brings us gratitude.
It's gratitude that brings us happiness."
— Anonymous

Today I Am Grateful For

_____

_____

_____

_____

_____

_____

_____

_____

_____

_____

_____

_____

_____

_____

_____

_____

_____

_____

"It's not happiness that brings us gratitude.
It's gratitude that brings us happiness."
— Anonymous

Today I Am Grateful For

"It's not happiness that brings us gratitude.
It's gratitude that brings us happiness."
— Anonymous

Today I Am Grateful For

_____

_____

_____

_____

_____

_____

_____

_____

_____

_____

_____

_____

_____

_____

_____

_____

_____

_____

_____

_____

"It's not happiness that brings us gratitude.
It's gratitude that brings us happiness."
— Anonymous

Today I Am Grateful For

_____

_____

_____

_____

_____

_____

_____

_____

_____

_____

_____

_____

_____

_____

_____

_____

_____

_____

_____

"It's not happiness that brings us gratitude.
It's gratitude that brings us happiness."
— Anonymous

Today I Am Grateful For

_____

_____

_____

_____

_____

_____

_____

_____

_____

_____

_____

_____

_____

_____

_____

_____

_____

_____

_____

_____

"It's not happiness that brings us gratitude.
It's gratitude that brings us happiness."
— Anonymous

Today I Am Grateful For

_____

_____

_____

_____

_____

_____

_____

_____

_____

_____

_____

_____

_____

_____

_____

_____

_____

_____

_____

"It's not happiness that brings us gratitude.
It's gratitude that brings us happiness."
— Anonymous

Today I Am Grateful For

_____

_____

_____

_____

_____

_____

_____

_____

_____

_____

_____

_____

_____

_____

_____

_____

_____

_____

_____

"It's not happiness that brings us gratitude.
It's gratitude that brings us happiness."
— Anonymous

Today I Am Grateful For

_____

_____

_____

_____

_____

_____

_____

_____

_____

_____

_____

_____

_____

_____

_____

_____

_____

_____

"It's not happiness that brings us gratitude.
It's gratitude that brings us happiness."
— Anonymous

Today I Am Grateful For

_____

_____

_____

_____

_____

_____

_____

_____

_____

_____

_____

_____

_____

_____

_____

_____

_____

_____

"It's not happiness that brings us gratitude.
It's gratitude that brings us happiness."
— Anonymous

Today I Am Grateful For

_____

_____

_____

_____

_____

_____

_____

_____

_____

_____

_____

_____

_____

_____

_____

_____

_____

_____

_____

"It's not happiness that brings us gratitude.
It's gratitude that brings us happiness."
— Anonymous

Today I Am Grateful For

_____

_____

_____

_____

_____

_____

_____

_____

_____

_____

_____

_____

_____

_____

_____

_____

_____

_____

_____

_____

"It's not happiness that brings us gratitude.
It's gratitude that brings us happiness."
— Anonymous

Today I Am Grateful For

_____

_____

_____

_____

_____

_____

_____

_____

_____

_____

_____

_____

_____

_____

_____

_____

_____

_____

_____

_____

"It's not happiness that brings us gratitude.
It's gratitude that brings us happiness."
— Anonymous

Today I Am Grateful For

_____

_____

_____

_____

_____

_____

_____

_____

_____

_____

_____

_____

_____

_____

_____

_____

_____

"It's not happiness that brings us gratitude.
It's gratitude that brings us happiness."
— Anonymous

Today I Am Grateful For

_____

_____

_____

_____

_____

_____

_____

_____

_____

_____

_____

_____

_____

_____

_____

_____

_____

_____

_____

_____

"It's not happiness that brings us gratitude.
It's gratitude that brings us happiness."
— Anonymous

Today I Am Grateful For

_____

_____

_____

_____

_____

_____

_____

_____

_____

_____

_____

_____

_____

_____

_____

_____

_____

_____

_____

"It's not happiness that brings us gratitude.
It's gratitude that brings us happiness."
— Anonymous

Today I Am Grateful For

_____

_____

_____

_____

_____

_____

_____

_____

_____

_____

_____

_____

_____

_____

_____

_____

_____

_____

_____

_____

"It's not happiness that brings us gratitude.
It's gratitude that brings us happiness."
— Anonymous

Today I Am Grateful For

_____

_____

_____

_____

_____

_____

_____

_____

_____

_____

_____

_____

_____

_____

_____

_____

_____

_____

_____

_____

_____

"It's not happiness that brings us gratitude.
It's gratitude that brings us happiness."
— Anonymous

Today I Am Grateful For

_____

_____

_____

_____

_____

_____

_____

_____

_____

_____

_____

_____

_____

_____

_____

_____

_____

_____

_____

"It's not happiness that brings us gratitude.
It's gratitude that brings us happiness."
— Anonymous

Today I Am Grateful For

_____

_____

_____

_____

_____

_____

_____

_____

_____

_____

_____

_____

_____

_____

_____

_____

_____

_____

"It's not happiness that brings us gratitude.
It's gratitude that brings us happiness."
— Anonymous

Today I Am Grateful For

_____

_____

_____

_____

_____

_____

_____

_____

_____

_____

_____

_____

_____

_____

_____

_____

_____

_____

_____

"It's not happiness that brings us gratitude.
It's gratitude that brings us happiness."
— Anonymous

Today I Am Grateful For

_____

_____

_____

_____

_____

_____

_____

_____

_____

_____

_____

_____

_____

_____

_____

_____

_____

_____

"It's not happiness that brings us gratitude.
It's gratitude that brings us happiness."
— Anonymous

Today I Am Grateful For

_____

_____

_____

_____

_____

_____

_____

_____

_____

_____

_____

_____

_____

_____

_____

_____

_____

_____

_____

"It's not happiness that brings us gratitude.
It's gratitude that brings us happiness."
— Anonymous

Today I Am Grateful For

_____

_____

_____

_____

_____

_____

_____

_____

_____

_____

_____

_____

_____

_____

_____

_____

_____

"It's not happiness that brings us gratitude.
It's gratitude that brings us happiness."
— Anonymous

Today I Am Grateful For

_____

_____

_____

_____

_____

_____

_____

_____

_____

_____

_____

_____

_____

_____

_____

_____

_____

_____

_____

_____

_____

"It's not happiness that brings us gratitude.
It's gratitude that brings us happiness."
— Anonymous

Today I Am Grateful For

_____

_____

_____

_____

_____

_____

_____

_____

_____

_____

_____

_____

_____

_____

_____

_____

_____

"It's not happiness that brings us gratitude.
It's gratitude that brings us happiness."
— Anonymous

Today I Am Grateful For

_____

_____

_____

_____

_____

_____

_____

_____

_____

_____

_____

_____

_____

_____

_____

_____

_____

_____

_____

"It's not happiness that brings us gratitude.
It's gratitude that brings us happiness."
— Anonymous

Today I Am Grateful For

_____

_____

_____

_____

_____

_____

_____

_____

_____

_____

_____

_____

_____

_____

_____

_____

_____

_____

"It's not happiness that brings us gratitude.
It's gratitude that brings us happiness."
— Anonymous

Today I Am Grateful For

_____

_____

_____

_____

_____

_____

_____

_____

_____

_____

_____

_____

_____

_____

_____

_____

_____

_____

_____

"It's not happiness that brings us gratitude.
It's gratitude that brings us happiness."
— Anonymous

Today I Am Grateful For

_____

_____

_____

_____

_____

_____

_____

_____

_____

_____

_____

_____

_____

_____

_____

_____

_____

_____

_____

"It's not happiness that brings us gratitude.
It's gratitude that brings us happiness."
— Anonymous

Today I Am Grateful For

"It's not happiness that brings us gratitude.
It's gratitude that brings us happiness."
— Anonymous

Today I Am Grateful For

_____
_____
_____
_____
_____
_____
_____
_____
_____
_____
_____
_____
_____
_____
_____
_____
_____
_____

"It's not happiness that brings us gratitude.
It's gratitude that brings us happiness."
— Anonymous

Today I Am Grateful For

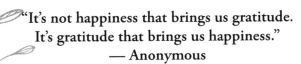

"It's not happiness that brings us gratitude.
It's gratitude that brings us happiness."
— Anonymous

Today I Am Grateful For

_____
_____
_____
_____
_____
_____
_____
_____
_____
_____
_____
_____
_____
_____
_____
_____
_____
_____
_____

"It's not happiness that brings us gratitude.
It's gratitude that brings us happiness."
— Anonymous

Today I Am Grateful For

_____

_____

_____

_____

_____

_____

_____

_____

_____

_____

_____

_____

_____

_____

_____

_____

_____

_____

_____

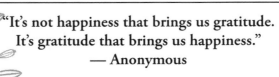

"It's not happiness that brings us gratitude.
It's gratitude that brings us happiness."
— Anonymous

Today I Am Grateful For

_____

_____

_____

_____

_____

_____

_____

_____

_____

_____

_____

_____

_____

_____

_____

_____

_____

_____

_____

"It's not happiness that brings us gratitude.
It's gratitude that brings us happiness."
— Anonymous

Today I Am Grateful For

_____

_____

_____

_____

_____

_____

_____

_____

_____

_____

_____

_____

_____

_____

_____

_____

_____

_____

_____

"It's not happiness that brings us gratitude.
It's gratitude that brings us happiness."
— Anonymous

Today I Am Grateful For

_____

_____

_____

_____

_____

_____

_____

_____

_____

_____

_____

_____

_____

_____

_____

_____

_____

_____

_____

"It's not happiness that brings us gratitude.
It's gratitude that brings us happiness."
— Anonymous

Today I Am Grateful For

_____

_____

_____

_____

_____

_____

_____

_____

_____

_____

_____

_____

_____

_____

_____

_____

_____

_____

"It's not happiness that brings us gratitude.
It's gratitude that brings us happiness."
— Anonymous

Today I Am Grateful For

_____

_____

_____

_____

_____

_____

_____

_____

_____

_____

_____

_____

_____

_____

_____

_____

_____

_____

_____

"It's not happiness that brings us gratitude.
It's gratitude that brings us happiness."
— Anonymous

Today I Am Grateful For

_____

_____

_____

_____

_____

_____

_____

_____

_____

_____

_____

_____

_____

_____

_____

_____

_____

"It's not happiness that brings us gratitude.
It's gratitude that brings us happiness."
— Anonymous

Today I Am Grateful For

_____

_____

_____

_____

_____

_____

_____

_____

_____

_____

_____

_____

_____

_____

_____

_____

_____

_____

_____

"It's not happiness that brings us gratitude.
It's gratitude that brings us happiness."
— Anonymous

Today I Am Grateful For

"It's not happiness that brings us gratitude.
It's gratitude that brings us happiness."
— Anonymous

Today I Am Grateful For

_____

_____

_____

_____

_____

_____

_____

_____

_____

_____

_____

_____

_____

_____

_____

_____

_____

_____

"It's not happiness that brings us gratitude.
It's gratitude that brings us happiness."
— Anonymous

Today I Am Grateful For

_____

_____

_____

_____

_____

_____

_____

_____

_____

_____

_____

_____

_____

_____

_____

_____

_____

"It's not happiness that brings us gratitude.
It's gratitude that brings us happiness."
— Anonymous

Today I Am Grateful For

_____

_____

_____

_____

_____

_____

_____

_____

_____

_____

_____

_____

_____

_____

_____

_____

_____

_____

"It's not happiness that brings us gratitude.
It's gratitude that brings us happiness."
— Anonymous

Today I Am Grateful For

_____

_____

_____

_____

_____

_____

_____

_____

_____

_____

_____

_____

_____

_____

_____

_____

_____

_____

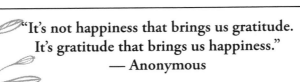

"It's not happiness that brings us gratitude.
It's gratitude that brings us happiness."
— Anonymous

Today I Am Grateful For

_____

_____

_____

_____

_____

_____

_____

_____

_____

_____

_____

_____

_____

_____

_____

_____

"It's not happiness that brings us gratitude.
It's gratitude that brings us happiness."
— Anonymous

88

Today I Am Grateful For

_____

_____

_____

_____

_____

_____

_____

_____

_____

_____

_____

_____

_____

_____

_____

_____

_____

_____

_____

"It's not happiness that brings us gratitude.
It's gratitude that brings us happiness."
— Anonymous

Today I Am Grateful For

_____

_____

_____

_____

_____

_____

_____

_____

_____

_____

_____

_____

_____

_____

_____

_____

_____

_____

_____

"It's not happiness that brings us gratitude.
It's gratitude that brings us happiness."
— Anonymous

Today I Am Grateful For

_____

_____

_____

_____

_____

_____

_____

_____

_____

_____

_____

_____

_____

_____

_____

_____

_____

_____

_____

"It's not happiness that brings us gratitude.
It's gratitude that brings us happiness."
— Anonymous

Today I Am Grateful For

_____

_____

_____

_____

_____

_____

_____

_____

_____

_____

_____

_____

_____

_____

_____

_____

_____

"It's not happiness that brings us gratitude.
It's gratitude that brings us happiness."
— Anonymous

Today I Am Grateful For

_____

_____

_____

_____

_____

_____

_____

_____

_____

_____

_____

_____

_____

_____

_____

_____

_____

_____

_____

_____

"It's not happiness that brings us gratitude.
It's gratitude that brings us happiness."
— Anonymous

Today I Am Grateful For

"It's not happiness that brings us gratitude.
It's gratitude that brings us happiness."
— Anonymous

Today I Am Grateful For

_____

_____

_____

_____

_____

_____

_____

_____

_____

_____

_____

_____

_____

_____

_____

_____

_____

_____

"It's not happiness that brings us gratitude.
It's gratitude that brings us happiness."
— Anonymous

Today I Am Grateful For

_____

_____

_____

_____

_____

_____

_____

_____

_____

_____

_____

_____

_____

_____

_____

_____

_____

_____

"It's not happiness that brings us gratitude.
It's gratitude that brings us happiness."
— Anonymous

Today I Am Grateful For

_____

_____

_____

_____

_____

_____

_____

_____

_____

_____

_____

_____

_____

_____

_____

_____

_____

_____

_____

_____

"It's not happiness that brings us gratitude.
It's gratitude that brings us happiness."
— Anonymous

Today I Am Grateful For

_____

_____

_____

_____

_____

_____

_____

_____

_____

_____

_____

_____

_____

_____

_____

_____

_____

"It's not happiness that brings us gratitude.
It's gratitude that brings us happiness."
— Anonymous

Today I Am Grateful For

_____

_____

_____

_____

_____

_____

_____

_____

_____

_____

_____

_____

_____

_____

_____

_____

_____

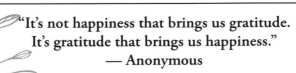

"It's not happiness that brings us gratitude.
It's gratitude that brings us happiness."
— Anonymous

Today I Am Grateful For

_____

_____

_____

_____

_____

_____

_____

_____

_____

_____

_____

_____

_____

_____

_____

_____

_____

_____

"It's not happiness that brings us gratitude.
It's gratitude that brings us happiness."
— Anonymous

Today I Am Grateful For

_____

_____

_____

_____

_____

_____

_____

_____

_____

_____

_____

_____

_____

_____

_____

_____

_____

_____

"It's not happiness that brings us gratitude.
It's gratitude that brings us happiness."
— Anonymous

Today I Am Grateful For

_____

_____

_____

_____

_____

_____

_____

_____

_____

_____

_____

_____

_____

_____

_____

_____

_____

_____

_____

_____

"It's not happiness that brings us gratitude.
It's gratitude that brings us happiness."
— Anonymous

Today I Am Grateful For

_____

_____

_____

_____

_____

_____

_____

_____

_____

_____

_____

_____

_____

_____

_____

_____

_____

_____

"It's not happiness that brings us gratitude.
It's gratitude that brings us happiness."
— Anonymous

Today I Am Grateful For

_____

_____

_____

_____

_____

_____

_____

_____

_____

_____

_____

_____

_____

_____

_____

_____

_____

_____

_____

_____

_____

"It's not happiness that brings us gratitude.
It's gratitude that brings us happiness."
— Anonymous

Today I Am Grateful For

_____

_____

_____

_____

_____

_____

_____

_____

_____

_____

_____

_____

_____

_____

_____

_____

_____

_____

_____

_____

"It's not happiness that brings us gratitude.
It's gratitude that brings us happiness."
— Anonymous

Today I Am Grateful For

_____

_____

_____

_____

_____

_____

_____

_____

_____

_____

_____

_____

_____

_____

_____

_____

"It's not happiness that brings us gratitude.
It's gratitude that brings us happiness."
— Anonymous

Today I Am Grateful For

_____

_____

_____

_____

_____

_____

_____

_____

_____

_____

_____

_____

_____

_____

_____

_____

_____

"It's not happiness that brings us gratitude.
It's gratitude that brings us happiness."
— Anonymous

Today I Am Grateful For

_____

_____

_____

_____

_____

_____

_____

_____

_____

_____

_____

_____

_____

_____

_____

_____

_____

_____

"It's not happiness that brings us gratitude.
It's gratitude that brings us happiness."
— Anonymous

Today I Am Grateful For

_____

_____

_____

_____

_____

_____

_____

_____

_____

_____

_____

_____

_____

_____

_____

_____

_____

_____

"It's not happiness that brings us gratitude.
It's gratitude that brings us happiness."
— Anonymous

Today I Am Grateful For

_____

_____

_____

_____

_____

_____

_____

_____

_____

_____

_____

_____

_____

_____

_____

_____

_____

_____

_____

"It's not happiness that brings us gratitude.
It's gratitude that brings us happiness."
— Anonymous

Today I Am Grateful For

_____

_____

_____

_____

_____

_____

_____

_____

_____

_____

_____

_____

_____

_____

_____

_____

_____

_____

_____

"It's not happiness that brings us gratitude.
It's gratitude that brings us happiness."
— Anonymous

Today I Am Grateful For

_____

_____

_____

_____

_____

_____

_____

_____

_____

_____

_____

_____

_____

_____

_____

_____

_____

_____

"It's not happiness that brings us gratitude.
It's gratitude that brings us happiness."
— Anonymous

Today I Am Grateful For

_____

_____

_____

_____

_____

_____

_____

_____

_____

_____

_____

_____

_____

_____

_____

_____

_____

_____

_____

"It's not happiness that brings us gratitude.
It's gratitude that brings us happiness."
— Anonymous

Today I Am Grateful For

_____

_____

_____

_____

_____

_____

_____

_____

_____

_____

_____

_____

_____

_____

_____

_____

_____

_____

_____

_____

"It's not happiness that brings us gratitude.
It's gratitude that brings us happiness."
— Anonymous

Today I Am Grateful For

"It's not happiness that brings us gratitude.
It's gratitude that brings us happiness."
— Anonymous

Today I Am Grateful For

_____

_____

_____

_____

_____

_____

_____

_____

_____

_____

_____

_____

_____

_____

_____

_____

_____

_____

_____

"It's not happiness that brings us gratitude.
It's gratitude that brings us happiness."
— Anonymous

Today I Am Grateful For

_____

_____

_____

_____

_____

_____

_____

_____

_____

_____

_____

_____

_____

_____

_____

_____

_____

_____

_____

_____

"It's not happiness that brings us gratitude.
It's gratitude that brings us happiness."
— Anonymous

Today I Am Grateful For

_____

_____

_____

_____

_____

_____

_____

_____

_____

_____

_____

_____

_____

_____

_____

_____

_____

_____

"It's not happiness that brings us gratitude.
It's gratitude that brings us happiness."
— Anonymous

Today I Am Grateful For

"It's not happiness that brings us gratitude.
It's gratitude that brings us happiness."
— Anonymous

Made in the USA
Columbia, SC
31 October 2022

70261909R00067